I0422056

Love Sports
Hate Politics

Just My Opinion

Rick L. Figg

Copyright © 2015 by Rick L. Figg.

| ISBN: | Softcover | 978-1-4990-4890-2 |
| | eBook | 978-1-4990-4889-6 |

All rights reserved. No part of this book may be reproduced or transmitted in any form or by any means, electronic or mechanical, including photocopying, recording, or by any information storage and retrieval system, without permission in writing from the copyright owner.

Any people depicted in stock imagery provided by Thinkstock are models, and such images are being used for illustrative purposes only.
Certain stock imagery © Thinkstock.

Print information available on the last page.

Rev. date: 09/17/2015

To order additional copies of this book, contact:
Xlibris
1-888-795-4274
www.Xlibris.com
Orders@Xlibris.com
650333

Contents

Dedication

This book is dedicated to my mother, the greatest person I have ever known—the all-time champion of mothers. I know a lot of people think they have the best mother, and they use phrases like "my mother's a saint." Well, my mommy truly is a saint, a disciple of love, an angel on earth—spreading her love and kindness and warmth to family, friends, and anyone and everyone she meets. She would see the good in people and bring it out of them by showing them she cares. Once she told me how she prayed for her children every day to be all right and that no harm will come to them. And you know, I could feel the protection that her prayers yielded; she is truly blessed and special. My four brothers and three sisters and I were raised with all the proper morals, humility, and respect to take care of ourselves and raise are children the same way. To be productive, responsible people with love and pride and a strong family bond. She gave me all I wanted and needed, and her goals of her family being happy were firmly accomplished. She was such a pleasant human being, a beautiful soul. I will miss her presence here on earth. I will always have my memories of her in my mind and in my heart and what she used to tell me that God loves us all. Love you champ, my mameo. Rest in peace to my family and friends gone on to glory in 2013—Aunt Daisy Partee, Spencer Johnson, Gilbert Perry, Wanda Watts, Jesse F1elds, Wilma Robinson, and my beloved mother Melzenie Figg.

Rickey Henderson

I played and went to school with some great athletes. A few made it to the pro and had great careers. The most successful is Rickey Henderson, an all-time major league stolen base king and hall of famer. We grew up in the same neighborhood, and we had the same school. I met him in fifth grade. He looked like a pro in junior high school football, baseball, basketball—he was real good at all of them. We were teammates in the high school football, the Oakland Tech Bulldogs. Rickey was our running back; he averaged 170 yards a game rushing and he was an all-city linebacker on defense. We were a running team that featured Rickey and we had another good back. J. Simmons he went to San Jose State. I was a receiver on the team—we had such a dynamic running attack; that's all we did, 300 yards per game on the ground. In a game against Oakland High, our coach, his name was Brooks. Coach Brooks called the same play over and over on one drive a running play to Rickey. The play was called I right twenty-four blast, he called it like eight or nine straight times, until we scored. We dominated that year—our running game with Rick was lethal; he was a force. He could run you over then run away from you with power and speed. In baseball when I said he looked like a pro, I really mean he looked like a pro. He was so polished and it was so natural; he looked like a man among boys with his skill level. I thought he would play football, but baseball was really the right decision. Rickey was really fast; he had great acceleration; when he could get up to full speed quickly, he was very fast but he was not the fastest guy on the football team. I was, not to brag or boast, but I was really fast back in the day. I know I was the fastest on the team. I was the fastest in school, but I stopped running during my sophomore year. Way back when it was yards not meters, I was clocking 9.2 and 9.3 in the hundred. Today I regret I stopped running. But anyway Rickey Henderson was a great all-around athlete. I heard his mother made the decision he would play baseball. Great choice, Mom; she called that right. I think he could have been a great running back in the NFL he just could not have played over fifteen seasons effectively like in baseball. Baseball's the right choice, especially for your body, it way less punishment; plus better salary, more longevity.

There has always been a history of good athletes out of our area back to Bill Russell, Paul Silas, Vada Pinson, Doc Shavers, Wolf Perry, Lloyd Moseby, Gary Pettis, Fred Atkins, Gary Payton, Jason Kidd, Leon Powe, MarShawn Lynch, Dammien Lilard, all from the Big O.

Love the Sports

Baseball in the inner city is no longer the place to find future stars because it doesn't exist. It has gradually dissipated over the last thirty years or so. A lot of the inner city players of the '60s, '70s, or the early '80s come from after-school sports programs. Cut away to the present where we have less after school sports, there are very few outlets recruiting the youth for these activities because there is no network, no series of organizations, no financing, and no plan.

You look at some of the areas where the Little League world series teams come from. Those teams and areas are rich in tradition from years of competition, and the parents are also heavily involved. Major League has a problem going from America's favorite pastime; now it's number three behind football and basketball. They have the RBI program that is sort of a crock because it does not go far or reach deep enough. They have a lot of work to do. One, when and where do you hear of this program? Where do they advertise? Where and how do they operate? How can they connect and or identify the places where the kids are. There is a lot of untapped, undeveloped talent out there. Major League baseball has fixated their operation the last thirty years or so in Latin America, supporting leagues and developing players from those countries, where the players are more hungry for baseball and where baseball does not compete with other sports, unlike in the US where football and basketball dominate. They need to bring that effort and enthusiasm back to the inner city, the ghetto, where when you give them baseball, they will take it. Growing up in the city of Oakland, sports was all we did—baseball season, baseball; football season, football; and basketball, all year-round. There were no video games or a lot of TV watching in the daytime. We were outside. Sports, a great occupier of time, creates camaraderie and bonding, sprit of competition, and generally kept us out of trouble. We formed our own teams by street, set up our own games. It was fun and organized; there was no fighting. Looking back now, I realize how special it was, how there was no type of violence. We just wanted to play. We would go at it 62nd Street vs. 63rd Street—basketball, football, baseball. My parents came up thru the Jackie Robinson era, watching him break the color line and into baseball made them love the sport. My mom loved the Dodgers, my Dad loved Willie Mays. I remember going to Giants Dodgers games as a little boy at Candlestick Park. As I got a little older, about eleven or twelve, my sister and I and a few friends started to go to the Oakland A's games by ourselves on the bus for 70 cents round-trip. In 1971, you could sit in the bleachers for a dollar fifty and behind the plate lower deck was six dollars, the best seats in the house. In 2013, the tickets are at least ten times more. Baseball, like all sports, are outpricing the average fan with eight-dollar hot dogs and ten-dollar beers. We could go to the game with twenty dollars and sit in the best seats eat all day and come home with a bunch of souvenirs, 50 cents for a hot dog, 25 cents for a large soda. We would get there two hours before the game to watch the players' pre-game warmup. Reggie Jackson, Vida Blue, Catfish Hunter, Joe Rudi, Sal Bando, Campy Campaneris, the swinging A's. The grass was so green, the field so perfect. The double headers were the best we would be at the ballpark all day long. Today in 2013, the now owners of the A's have been trying to move the team out of town because of its location from the edge of East Oakland they want to move to a more affluent area where the big money is closer to the Silicon Valley. So they don't promote the team locally around the area where the stadium is the A's used to go out in the community more, advertise promotion, offer free or discount tickets to local residents in the immediate areas. And now their excuse for leaving can be see the people won't come out and support the team. They can build a stadium on the location there at now if they wanted to, but they won't. On the field, the money ball thing is effective, but it's hard to get to the World Series if you continue to have a fire sale every year, with players trading some of the pieces that would get you to the level. Seems like they got rid of a good pitcher and the next year they need a good pitcher. Right the one you just traded off your team. The A's have a lot of fight and grit and good coaching they also play very hard, they have continued to show up in the playoffs in the recent seasons no matter whom they have on the field. I am a Bay Area sports fan. I support all the teams— 49ers, Raiders, A's, Giants, Warriors, Cal, Stanford, the Sharks. They say you can't be a Raider fan and a 49ers fan. I say you can because I am. I love football. The Raiders was my number one team, then they moved left and went to LA; they lost me after that. I'm all in on the 49ers.

The Oakland Raiders in the '60s and the '70s, you mention the city of Oakland and the first thing people thought about was the Black Panthers, the Hells Angles, and the Oakland Raiders. They kind of fall right in line—radical group, radical team, all of them with an edge—they were different. They were a true commitment to excellence. Going to a Raider game was a great experience: the silver and black, the tailgating, the crowd, the electric atmosphere. And it was like the Raiders won most of their games; always playoffs, always in the hunt. I was at a playoff game against the Pittsburgh Steelers the year the Raiders beat the Vikings in the Superbowl. The coliseum was wild—it was loud, it was crazy, the building was moving. All the fans there knew the Raiders were going to win at the kickoff, it was destiny. I mean poetic like John Facenda NFL films-type stuff. And after all that, they decided to move—ain't that bitch. I loved the team because it is my home team. Wow, what a shocker after years of straight sellouts and the most loyal fans in the world betrayed. Then they moved to LA where they went to the Superbowl their first year there. That year, they practiced and lived in the Bay Area and made the forty-five-minute flight to LA to play. No distractions from Hollywood living in the Bay Area kept them focused they got to the Superbowl and beat Washington, another slap in the face, they win as the LA Raiders not Oakland. After that, they moved the total operation to LA; the players all moved and they settled in. After that, everything went right down the toilet—they lost their identity. After several losing seasons, they moved back to Oakland and they have been searching for that glory ever since. The fans slowly came back, there was a difference. It was a lot of new Raiders fans. Some of these fans missed the grandfathering in the introduction of the pre-LA Raider fans. They have great enthusiasm but their approach is different. They thought they had to have a *thugs* mentality, over-the-top aggression that plagued the game with over-zealous attacking people in opposing jerseys, creating a rowdy environment. Not to say that all new Raider fans are that way. The Raider nation has the most loyal fans, the best fans, but you only need a few to fuck it up for everyone. With your home team, the team you support, there are some bad moments. One of the worst for me as a Raider fan was the immaculate reception. I was just a kid watching in my pajamas; it was one of those early games and I remember how a freak play was so disappointing I mean it hurt. I was mad for like five years over that one play, it was unbelievable. The Raiders were about to win the game, they shut the Steelers out on the previous downs the D line was chasing Bradshaw around. He was under all kinds of pressure, the DB's were locking up the receivers, Bradshaw flings a desperation prayer right to Jack Tatum who knocks the ball to the ground so it seems. All of a sudden, Franco Harris is running and he got the football headed for the end zone. Pittsburghs crowd is going nuts, he scores a touchdown game over Steelers win. Now out of all the angles of the film footage and the replay, you never really see Harris catch the ball. You just see him reaching for it and running. To this day, I am still not convinced he caught the ball before it hit the ground. There was a lesson I learned at an early age. You got to let it go, you can be upset over loses but don't hold on to it. After all, it's just sports, as long as you live to play another day, life goes on.

Football

Football—the game is a monster; it's a very hard tough game. How do you tame a monster that you can't even contain? Hard to regulate because of the nature collision crash bang men between 200 and 360 pounds, running into each other at full speed. Hard plastic helmets and pads, muscle and sweat, the helmet and shoulder pads—they are weapons as well as protection. You know the helmet and pads have evolved with the game, so the helmet went from protection to a weapon check. The history was that the helmet started as leather, with no face mask. Now helmets are made of the hardest plastic poly urethane and face mask that look like they belong on a gladiator's helmet meets Star Wars. Today, the NFL is trying to rain in the hard-hitting blows to the head. The only thing the game is beyond that there is helmet to helmet on every play. If you want to get technical, the biggest guys on the field go head to head on every play the lineman have instant collision. It's a rough, tough game, and you know that from pee wee or when you get your first taste of tackle as a kid that there are some risks of getting hurt. We know that but we enthusiastically play on because we want that.

Speaking of hard hits, the hardest hitter I have ever seen to this day was the Oakland Raider Jack Tatum. No one could lay the pads on people better than Tatum. He could hit so hard and clean; with that shoulder, he could launch and hit with pinpoint accuracy. If he wanted to hit you in the head, he would or he could blast any part of the body—torso, legs, whatever was open. Tatum got a bad rep after the Darryl Stingley incident and his book *They Call Me Assassin*. Some people backed away from him, and his legacy and reputation was tarnished. No hall of fame and no real recognition and acknowledgment of his playing career. The fact is to me that he was a great player and was a perfect example of a strong safety. Jack Tatum was a force, stopping the run and pass. His game was intimidation; the receivers and backs knew Jack Tatum was lurking his thing, was knocking off helmets. I remember him doing that a lot. Earl Cambell had a rep for running over people—a big powerful back about 235 Tatum took him on at the goal line and smack the hell out of him. Cambell fell forward into the end zone for the touchdown and did not get up. He had to be helped off the field; he scored but he paid for it. Jack Tatum—the best ever; with the shoulder pads, he would give you a jolt. Today he would rack up a lot of fines. A player like Dick (Night Train) Lane wouldn't last today. His favorite tackle was the clothesline, that's how bad he was. Players today are starting to make the adjustment to the new strike zone rules. They are gauging what they can do. We know overt head strikes and head targeting is out; everything else also questionable, and there is a different rule and zone for quarterbacks. You got quarterback in the pocket, you got quarterbacks running, you got quarterbacks sliding. You have to watch out for their knee, their heads, and don't tackle them hard and definitely don't drive them into the ground. When I was a kid watching a Raider Colts game, Big Bubba Smith sacked Darryl Lamonica. When I say sacked, I mean he *picked him up*, and piled drive him into the turf with his full body weight on him. Bubba was 6'7" at 300 pounds. Needless to say, Lamonica did not throw another pass that day—he was done. That move today would catch a huge fine and suspension and full blast scrutiny from the media and outrage from the fans and the league. It would have been damn near criminal. Boy, how things have changed. Bottom line is you can't knock the shit out of people these days. When we first practiced organized football pee wee high school, all the same the coaches have the drill with the big hanging hitting bag. They walk you up to it and teach you how to launch using the crown of your helmet, driving your fist into the ball carriers chest using your legs as you explode into the tackle. Wow, they taught you to use your helmet in blocking and tackling.

So now we have to start teach the new proper hitting technique in this millennium. Hey, the way before was not wrong; that's just how it was. One thing I know about football is that your head and your heart have to be on it when you're playing it at any level. Risks—you don't care about risk if you love to play. As a parent, I let my kids make that decision. Parents who chose otherwise, find your kid a baseball team if you can.

The 49ers

The 49ers, yeah, that's my team. I claim, I ride, I roll with them for forty years. I remember John Brodie QB when I was a kid; they played at Candlestick. I don't remember them playing at Kezar, but I do remember watching them grow to a power and win five Superbowl rings, build a legacy of a great team hall of fame players and coach, and a string of seventeen straight playoff appearances— from the catch to the rise of the Kaep from Bill Walsh, Joe Montana, Jerry Rice, the drafting of Ronnie Lott, the heart and soul of the championship defense, to Patrick Willis and Navarro Bowman and the smiths Aldon and Justin wreaking havoc. The dynasty that started in the '80's with Eddie DeBartolo brought in Bill Walsh, they put together a winning organization. We know how they set the standard on a blueprint on how to build a dynasty. Today, bringing back the championship pedigree in the Harbaugh era and the York family connection ownership and management excellence. The 49ers have been at the top of the NFC for the last three years with one trip to the Superbowl. The team looks strong-primed to make a run for the next four or five years they will get that sixth ring soon. I got enough 49er history for a whole book—that's next.

Wow, what a season! Coach Jim Harbaugh gone, Patrick Willis forced to retire, Frank Gore with the Colts. Star rookie linebacker retires from concussion scare, Mike Impati gone to division rival Cardinals, defense dismantled, coaching staff blown up. All that happened end of 2014 season. As a fan, hearing all the rumblings all season combined with the 49ers' performance, changes were expected, to what extreme we will all find out after the smoke clears and the dust settles. Where we stand, the 49ers will either be at the bottom of the division or surprise people and rebuild quickly. Anyway, I am not worried the 49ers will rise again, as they always do.

The Sports 2

I find sports refreshing; it is live and spontaneous—the ultimate reality show. You know it's real. You have people enforcing the rules—referees, umpires—everything is regulated and regimented. The competition, the sprit each individual or team creates, accelerating moments, and lasting memories; men, women, and children all can participate in sports at any level, from pee wee to the pros, for a weekend recreation, whatever you do participating expecting it's fun. You can call it a hobby or just something to do. Through my lifetime, it is a part of me. It has grown to where I really enjoy it. Football season, I'm all in; basketball, the same. I love sports but that's me part of a large fraternity of sports fans. I remember watching ESPN when it first came on the air. There was a buildup about a twenty-four-hour sports station starting sports all day, all night. My friends and I were excited sport twenty-four hours, seven days a week, Chris Berman, Tom Mees, Bob Lee, it was college sports, a lot of rugby late at night, and of course, sports center. Today, it's the undisputed king. It owns sports news and entertainment owned by conglomerate institutional giant Disney, who owns ABC, which made so big and bad they swooped in Monday night football. The sports leader no doubt, they already had the NBA and major league baseball, which also led to in-depth reporting of sports, not just ESPN. Fox has a twenty-four hour sports network NBA, NFL, MLB they all have networks CBS, NBC, all have huge sports divisions. Throw in cable and the Internet, and pod cast radio shows adds up to a powerful sports media where everyone is looking for the top story in the twenty-four hour news cycle, and it can get vicious. If regular news was like sports news, we would know everything. It all would be exposed politicians wouldn't stand a chance; they would turn over every rock. Sports news looks for on the field and off the field drama. They investigate, expose, and uncover. There are more leaks in sports and its governing organization than the federal government remotely has. Every controversial story starts with an unnamed source then all of a sudden, the so-called confidential information that was not to be released gets released because somebody leaked it. I don't know if people are getting paid or just have no loyalty or what the motivation is. If you have signed agreement legal not to release information that's how it's should be, right? No one ever questions the leaker of such information and the legality of it because they are looking for the end result and that is to get the target individuals implicated. A whistle blower is different from a leaker; whistle blowers have different motivations. A leaker is looking to get paid. Yeah, if real news was like sports news, it would be wild. I get more real news from the daily show with Jon Stewart and that ain't no joke. I love basketball; the NBA college at tournament time, college ball was better in the '70s or '80s and the ''90s. The players were better because they stayed three or four years. You could better assess how a player would play in the pros when you can see how they progressed through college. I still have vivid memories of Lorenzo Charles grabbing Dereck Whittenburg's last shot attempt and dunking it to win the game for NC State, the underdog. That team had something special—they were gritty and they hustled and they never gave up. Other memories of Keith Smart hitting the baseline jumper for Indiana almost from the same spot whereMichael Jordan hit his game sealer for North Carolina. The list of great players goes on: Magic Johnson, Isaiah Thomas, Carl Malone, Charles Barkley, and the diesel big Shaq. There was one player I noticed when I was a kid, he made me pay attention to basketball. He came out of New York, his name was Lew Alcindor. He goes to UCLA and changed the landscape of college basketball. At 7'1" with leaping ability, he dunked easy and all the time when he was close to the basket. He was so good at dunking he started the "no dunking allowed" rule in college basketball. That's how dominant he was. They deemed it an unfair advantage, so Alcindor adjusted and goes to a series of soft layups and hook shots around the hoop very effectively, still unstoppable. So actually the NCAA outlawing the dunk was key in Alcindor, now Kareem Abdul-Jabbar, in developing his famous hook shot. The NBA develops great rivalries and comparisons: Wilt vs. Russel, Magic vs. Bird Celts, Lakers Bulls, Pistons. The Jordan-LeBron thing! Michael Jordan is the greatest basketball player I have seen in my lifetime. I would say Magic is number two. There are a lot of great players behind them; everyone has their own opinions in what order. LeBron James is coming, his career is far from over. We have to wait to see how he finishes his career before we know where he lands. People today are always making the comparison between MJ and LBJ; they really are hard to compare because they are different players. LBJ is a physical specimen 6'8" 260 pounds locomotive, with the speed of a guard and the strength of a power forward—a cross between Magic and Carl Malone, a force unstoppable going to the hoop big and fast supreme defender great passer, all the tools that add up to a superior basketball player. MJ 6'6" 225 pounds prototype big guard, extra smooth, quick, with the leaping ability to stop and pop in the air like he was on a trampoline. When Jordan comes at you on the dribble drive, he is giving you the schoolyard fakes jump cuts and a whole series of moves on his way to the basket. Now here's the difference, the thing about Jordan is he can get a shot off and score on two, three, four, five people, and he also was a willing passer when he is covered, and that is the difference. LBJ does not look to score in those situations; when doubled and tripled he will make the pass instinctively. He is still writing his story. They both can take over a game on both ends. MJ has six rings. I don't rate *could* and *should*. If you do that with MJ, he *could* have won eight maybe nine straight and that *would* put the whole greatest argument away forever, when you factor in the two years he took off to play baseball. Also the year after they won number six, when the Bulls let go of Phil Jackson and dismantled the team, that was a chance for number nine. How stupid was that. It's ironic the Bulls are still making weird moves today, trading Dang for Andrew Bynum and then releasing him, that's a different story. I've watched a lot of players come and go in the last thirty years or so in the NBA as they start their careers and they end them like Magic Johnson. The reason I choose Magic as number two is because the way he changed the game and he was a winner. A 6'9" point guard that ran the fast break better than anyone. Magic end-to-end showtime for real. They would say about Magic, if you're his teammate, you better be ready for the pass because if you are not ready, he will bust you upside the head with the ball. He could take you out with one of his gilded missile rocket passes—best passer ever. I saw him once throw a full court bounce pass right on the money to Michael Cooper in stride for a dunk—incredible. He also was what I call a scoreboard watcher. What I mean is he always watches the score where he made sure his team was always in the lead. This is very important for a point guard, a leader knowing when it's time for a basket to knock opponents out. Magic came into the league, won five rings, and brought new excitement to the game; with the epic battles with Larry Bird of Celtics, they took the league to a new level.

The Doctor Julius Erving, the first f lyer that I knew as a fan. Before I actually saw the Doc play, I heard a lot about him. He played in the ABA; they were not on TV. There was talk of a player that could sky he could dunk taking off from the foul line and could glide to the hoop hanging in the air, defying gravity. I remember watching the highlights of a red, white, and blue ball, and an afro flying back being cleared for take off. I could see a long arm extended gripped by a massive hand up at least a foot up over the basket, dunking in Bill Walton's face. I was also watching the game against the Lakers, where Doc went down the baseline, came around the behind the basket, extended the arm, and scooped the ball in the basket with English. All I know when Doc was doing that move, I was saying, *where is the Doc going with that move?* He is going to be forced out of bounds and then he proceeded to defy gravity—twisting, floating, hanging in the air—incredible! The Doctor, my first favorite superstar basketball player. The Doc has the huge hands that could palm the ball; he could jump up and finger roll eye level at the rim; or dunk it with his elbows damn near inside the basket. His classic highlight dunk against the Lakers on Michael Cooper is timeless. The rock the cradle and the wind up and over the top follow thru slam, what a great in game dunk. The funny thing was how the Doc sized Cooper up before he threw down and how Cooper at first started to go for the block and then thought better of it and decided to become a spectator as he ducked his head as the ball ripped through the net—priceless! I give respect to the players who were a little before my time, and I barely saw them at the tail ends of their careers. Bill Russell, the greatest winner ever with eleven championships, and Wilt Chamberlain, the most dominant player. Wilt scored 100 points in a game, he also had a season where he averaged 50 points per game; in another game, he had 55 rebounds, and in another game, he blocked 26 shots. Now all of that is just mind-blowing dominating to that level 100 points in a game. When will you think you would ever see that again? Probably never. One of those unbreakable records, like in baseball, no one will ever get a hit in 56 straight games like Joe DiMaggio, and no one will score over 200 touchdowns in their career like the great Jerry Rice.

Boxing

The history of boxing and the black community goes a long way. Boxing is the first sport a black man could get famous in, rich in, win a title in, and get respect in. Jack Johnson stood defiant in a time where being defiant could get you killed or locked away in jail. Later, Joe Louis loved by blacks and whites; a symbol of pride for blacks whites gravitated when he fought the German Smelling. The Sugar Ray Robinson era in the '40s and '50s was more lucrative and more barriers came down. Watching Floyd Mayweather take apart Carmelo Alvarez, while giving him a real boxing lesson, makes me think back to some of the great fights like Ali-Frazier 1, 2 and 3; Ali-Foreman; several good Sugar Ray Leonard fights; and Mike Tyson's devastating knock-out streak. Roberto Duran's hands of stone; Aaron Pryor's relentless Julio Cesar Chavez winning streak, these are just a small part of a litany of great fighters. The best fight I ever saw has to be the three rounds of hell between Hagler and Hearns, nonstop action, a punch fest each man going at it, giving all they had, incredible unbelievably brutal pace trying to impose their will toe to toe. It was spectacular boxing at its peak. The luster of the fight game is far from what it was in the past. One reason is a lot of the athletes

turn their attentions to more popular sports. Football, for example.

The potential heavyweight champion is a linebacker on some pro

football team. MMA, that's a whole different thing, you can punch,

kick, choke, stomp, throw elbow, wrestle, and submit with a series

of arm bars, leg locks—it's very close to no-holds-barred street fight

with a referee. And, of course, boxing has the strict Marques of

Queensberry rules. Mike Tyson spoiled us with the big knockout; he

made us a bit blood thirsty. The thrill, the devastation, the shock of

the quick one-punch knockout, which also led to the fascination with

the MMA because of the chance of the big knockout, the unpadded

gloves, the use of the knees and the elbows all add up to devastating

knockouts. Yeah, Mike Tyson did it. Boxing was the gateway to

success, a way out for a lot of young black men from the beginning

of the century all the way up until the '80s, as African Americans

start to dominate other sports, baseball, basketball, and football,

college athletics and the pros took all the hunger out of boxing. The

thing is boxing still captivates the African American audience and

it still is a great unifier when there is a great champion. Today there

are a few Mayweather, Andre Ward, and a couple more who are not

household names. Roy Jones for a stretch has incredible speed power,

grace. Sugar Ray Leonard was the same; he could hit people with a barrage of power punches in a matter of seconds. Marvelous Marvin Hagler could walk through guys. Nobody could throw the left hook better than smokin' Joe Frazier. Larry Holmes had a jab like a piston, followed with the textbook right hand over the top. Ridick Bowe was great when he was motivated. The will of Evander Holyfield, the rise of the Sphinx brothers, the first and second coming of George Foreman and his punching power, and Muhammad Ali's biggest fight with the federal government stripping him of his title. Don King and Bob Arum, the builders and destroyers of the product, their monopoly and power struggle stifled the growth of boxing for years. Borderline crooks manipulating fighters, ask Mike Tyson. There has not been a heavyweight champ from the US in a long time. That guy is probably a linebacker in the NFL today, that's where the talent pool has migrated to, long gone are the days of Tyson, Riddick Bowe, and Holyfield. The Klitchcos have dominated and I hate to say weak uninspired crop of US heavyweights. Floyd Mayweather runs the game in his divisions. We need a heavyweight champ like that with the current prospects we may never see it. How many people know who the top heavyweight contender from the US, I don't.

The Warriors

The Warriors, my home team, moved to the Bay Area in 1962. They were called the San Francisco Warriors. My understanding was that because Oakland had an ABA team, the Oakland Oaks, there was an agreement with the NBA merger that if the NBA team came to the area, they would play in Oakland, so that's when they came up with the name Golden State representing the Bay Area and Northern California. Here are some of my first recollection of the Warriors when I was a kid. They were led by Rick Barry, a great player dead-eye jump shooter, always played hard. He was a leader and that special underhand free-throw style where he shot over 90 percent for his career. They had good players: Phil Smith, Nate Thurmond, Clifford Ray, Jamaal Wilkes, and coach Al Attles with the fu man chu mustache. The year they won it all, beating Washington with the rotation they used, Coach Attles used ten players on that championship run. Their owner, Franklin Mulley, with his Sherlock Holmes hat was a colorful character, and they were a fun team then it kind of reminds me of the team today with the camaraderie team play and great coaching. After that's said, it has been some disappointing years—trade blunders, questionable draft choices, and bad front office moves. The Bernard King thing, the Joe Barry Carrol mistake, the Chris Webber debacle, the Tim Hardaway what a waste, the Mitch Richmond trade, what the f#@k, sugar Ray Richardson, huh? The Patrick Ewing lottery, the ownership kept firing duds with more bad news. Bernard King had resurrected his career in the Bay Area. Warriors fans already knew how good he was before he went to New York and blew up. We already knew he could score on anyone; Warriors fans knew when Bernard got the ball, he went to work with his array of shot around the bucket turnarounds, floaters push shots, the whole repertoire. When he started rolling, he was unstoppable. But instead of the Warriors trying to keep him, they have to trade him for Sugar Ray Richardson, huh? Richardson was a decent point guard, no disrespect. Bernard King was a great player; Richardson was nowhere near him. I could not believe they let him get away, a bonehead move, and that was just one of them; we got plenty more. Check this one out: the Warriors traded up to get the first pick in the draft; the first pick projected was Joe Barry Carrol, seven-foot center, best center coming out of college supposedly. Low post player good offensively. So they make the trade; they trade their current center Robert Parrish and their pick which was number two to the Celtics. With that pick, they take the player the Warriors would have taken if they stayed at that; spot that player was Kevin McHale. So the Warriors traded Robert the chief Parrish and one of the best power forwards of all time to the Celtics to team up on the frontline with Larry Bird. So therefore the Warriors are the architect of that part of the Celtics dynasty. And I don't even remember what happened to Joe Barry Carrol. I think he ended up in Houston, I'm not sure, but the bottom line: it is one of the worst trades of all time; the worst trade ever.

Hold it, not finished yet. The lottery before the NBA lottery, it was the team that had the worst record automatically got the first pick. That year, they decided to change it. That year, Patrick Ewing was the number one rated player coming out of college. The Warriors had the worst record by far, but they still had to go through the lotto for the pick order even though the odds were so-called in their favor because of the percentage of ping pong balls in their name. And we all know now the first pick went to the Knicks, the seventh pick went to the Warriors; if the old rules were in effect, the Knicks would have had the seventh pick because of their record. The Warriors drafted Chris Mullin who turned out to be a pretty good player but the Warriors still got reamed they could of had in the West changed the whole balance of the league. Now that one

I can't blame on the Warriors. The league screwed them on that. Some say the fix was in New York basketball needing a boost by sending Ewing to the Knicks and it was. Conspiracy? Who knows. Don Nelson the good the bad and the Nellie. Now Nelson did bring respectability back and an exciting brand of basketball with his stints as Warriors coach. He could build a team up and he could dismantle one too. I liked Nellie and most Warriors fans did also. Chris Cohen owned the team; he gave Nellie player and personnel power that may have been too much, some very questionable moves may have damaged the team. The Mitch Richmond trade for the rookie Billy King. And after they draft Chris Webber; he has a great first season, rookie of the year helped turn the team around. It turned out there is a problem between Webber and Nellie—they can't get along—and after one season they traded him for Tom Gugliotta. Wow, that was crazy and out of the blue. Nellie traded one of his best young players out of spite, I guess. Nellie, he tried to explain it but it never made sense to me. And then came a slew of bad decisions trading Tim Hardaway, a horrible deal; Chris Mullen goes to the Pacers; TMC dismantled; oh yeah, almost forgot draft day trade the rights for Vince Carter for Antawn Jamison. After all of that, Nellie comes back for another stint, rebuilt the team, and made it back to the playoffs, and upset the Mavericks, Nellie's former team, in the first round the Baron Davis led team Monte Ellis was like a one man fast break Warriors make a big trade midseason to turn their season around.

Bringing in Steven Jackson and Al Harrington, that team played together and made a lot of noise, scared some people, they ended up losing to Utah. When they were on this divine mission with Derek Fisher, he gets off the plane, shows up at half time after his daughter's eye surgery, and played out of his mind like he was on a mission and lifted the Jazz to victory and on to the next round. Warrior playoff appearances were few and far between. There is one playoff win I recall more vividly than the others; it was the one Eric Sleepy Floyd went for 57 against the Lakers; yeah, the Magic Johnson, Kareem Lakers. Sleepy scored 29 in one quarter; it's like he could not miss. He was making every shot and the funny thing was the Lakers were all over him; they were scrambling and chasing all over the court, and he was killing them with drives to the hoop jumpers from all angles, everything was falling. I remember looking at Sleepy's eyes and they called him Sleepy because he looked like he was sleepy; his eyes were kind of droopy. But not that day, his eyes were wide open like wild like buck wild. His focus was so intense and he was going wherever he wanted to go. He was on fire he had at least four or five guys at him all the time and he was just swishing shots in the

Lakers' face—one of the most incredible barrage of scoring I have ever seen. Yeah, Sleepy was wide awake that night he lit it up. Now the Warriors today, they are on a new mission after that last Don Nelson on the playoff run fueled by Barron Davis. And I do miss Monte Ellis. He gave us all he had as a warrior; he is still one of my favorite players. Good luck in Dallas . . . The Warrior has rebuilt with the most dynamic sharp shooters in the league. Stephen Curry, that dude can play. He is dangerous, deadly, whatever adjective you want to use for shooting lights out. He can break you down off the dribble drive to the basket shoot floaters, finger rolls, bank shots, and splash three-pointers from anywhere. And on top of all that, he is a great passer. He is the best player and floor leader. David Lee is solid great player; he takes guys to school on and off the low block. Klay Thompson, good shooter good defender; Andre Iguodala, glue guy utility can do anything, versatile; and Andrew Bogut in the middle with his length. They have a great coach in Mark Jackson. They play hard and they are exciting; their problem right now is their bench, no fire power that's consistent, and the big guys coming off the bench are hurt; no Festus; no Jermaine O'Neal. Draymond is good and Harrison Barnes has to get adjusted to coming off the bench. With all of that, they will make the playoffs. Where they'll go is yet to be seen. Go Warriors.

As of this day, the Warriors are in first place in the west, on the way to the playoffs folks, but the Warriors look scary good. They are blowing teams out playing, them like a well-oiled machine—passing, shooting, playing defense, flying around—all in sync. Coach Mark Jackson is gone replaced by Coach Steve Kerr who is pressing all the right buttons. Jackson molded this group, gave them character, confidence attitude, and a high-energy, hustling defensive identity to compete and win at the highest level. That is all the product of Coach Mark Jackson. Steve Kerr has come in and done everything right, the best job possible. He has taken players that were ready to grow and step up to the next level, and so far he gets an A plus. All I have to say now is that the Golden State Warriors do very well this season. NBA championship to the Bay Area.

Women and Football

There are four kinds of women you deal with relating to football. First, the kind who hates football and most sports. She hates that you watch, she hates that you like it, and she will do anything to keep you from watching it. They don't like it because they don't understand it. The game has a lot of rules it can be confusing at times. When they do let you watch it, they try to make you feel some type of guilt for watching it. I know it sounds weird but it happens. They make it seem like you prefer sports over them. My answer is, not all the time (just playing).

Second, they are the ones who try to like it, but they really don't. But they will let you watch, and they understand that is what you do, so they roll with it.

Third, they are the type who like football and will watch it and generally like sports but she is not on the level or as into it as much as you or as passionate, but she understands.

Fourth, is my favorite type. The one-in-a-million kind who loves the game as much as you do. I'm talking about she got a fantasy football team. Sunday, Monday, and Thursday are football days. She is enthusiastic when football season starts and sad when the season ends. She gets up Sunday and turns on the Redzone. She loves the home team just as much as you do, and she feels the same about the NBA. That's the grand prize jackpot. That is really so simple yet so deep. If you think about it, how just having that in common can improve a relationship. Football ladies, that's the way to your man's heart, wow, what a concept. Try it, it couldn't hurt.

On the other hand, if she doesn't like football or any other sports and wants to go shopping or looking for antiques, I respect that just because of the fact that I respect her choice and what she enjoys and makes her happy, and I expect she will do the same for me. Besides after watching sports for over thirty-five years, it's hard to stop.

The Lines

I want my sports inside the lines not outside. I want to see and be a part of the play on the court or on the field. I want to judge that athlete on strictly what he or she does on the field between the lines. I don't need to know if he is having marriage problems or he got a speeding ticket or even a DUI as long as no one was hurt. I don't care if he pays alimony or child support, or if they are estranged from their parents—it's not my business and anyway, those are just regular people problems. Star athletes are human beings too. They have a life too, believe it or not. I just want to evaluate them on the court on their performance in their chosen athletic profession. As long as they don't kill, rape, steal, or assault, I'm good. Those are laws you can't break; they're just wrong.

If it happens on the field, that's all I want to be concerned about. But unfortunately those lines get crossed. Player's personalities and attitudes are factored in. I really don't care about who Tiger Woods is dating and his relationship with his wife. And I don't give a shit about Manti Te'o's girlfriend—boy, what a major waste of time that was. At times, I think it's overkill and they start to turn over every rock, sometimes creating a circus atmosphere. Let's make a big jump to PEDs, the dreaded steroids, you know, I don't care. I don't care who used it then and who uses it now. We really have no proof. Most of these people never failed a drug test. All we really have is a lot of allegations, finger pointing, he said he said, outright denial as well as anger, shock, righteous indignation. You got your positive test, your tainted test, your leaked test, confirmed test, unconfirmed test. You got Jose Conseco and Bud Selig, and everyone in between. You got Barry Bonds who was a hall of famer before all that started and now can't even get a whiff of the hall or the fame. They don't want to even acknowledge his season and lifetime homerun records. Barry Bonds put on the greatest display of hitting ever; yes, ever. His strike zone was the size of a grapefruit. He was impossible to strike out. His ability to make contact extraordinary. He was locked in, the pitchers were afraid to throw him strikes. He had a record season for walks as they pitched around him in fear. He is to me the best baseball player I have ever seen, hands down. The way that Bonds put the bat on the ball for years and especially the record season was phenomenal. There were line shots he was dialed in perfect technique, arms extended follow through driving off the back leg, generating power swings, the kind of swing you learn from repetition, proper mechanics, and over seventeen years of experience and hand-eye coordination off the chart. I know a great player when I see one. Barry Bonds was one. Rodger Clemens, Sammy Sosa, Mark McGwire happened, and apparently MLB has problems proving allegations. So let's move along and let time heal some of these wounds and solve some problems. And let Barry Bonds in the hall of fame for what we saw him do on the field. A-Rod was dead meat; he was going down. They were after him like the FBI was after Capone. They brought in this Bosch character—he just reeked of a rat that has caused a plague. He is like the lowest form of rodent, like low enough to play handball against the curb; so low he could crawl under a rat like under the hoodrat, a carburetor transmission rat (get it?) hood like a car, but the other thing anyway, the dude is beyond sleazy. Is it true he was compensated five million dollars for his cooperation? They bailed him out with the IRS, jail time several criminal charges, bankruptcy, and a failing business; so he actually sold them. A-Rod served him up on a platter. What about the guy who originally took the paperwork, the files on A-Rod, MLB offered him $125,000 for the documents and he turned it down. Later, someone broke in his car and stole the documents that subsequently landed in the hands of MLB. So the question is did MLB rip off, yes, rob, the original guy who had the documents first? I mean who do they think they are? The CIA running covert ops. I'm just saying something is funny. Say if Babe Ruth had a weight trainer and worked out, you think he would have been an even better player; or if he had the technology to look at a high-speed slow motion digital breakdown frame by frame of his swing, so he can correct it, you think he could improve his swing or his batting stance? What if Hank Aaron or Willie Mays on the Nautilus machine working with Tim Grover year-round, you think they would have been even better players? Sports science and sports technology have and away will create advantages if you want to get technical. The evolution of sports and science has accelerated leaps and bounds in the last few decades, and the athletes are better because they work out all year-round, weight training and diet. What benefits can steroids yield? We know they can help with the healing process in some cases. Let's find out what all the effects are to protect the players from themselves. Science won't stop. They will come up with a drug in the future that will be undetectable. The thing that's ironic is that back in the '90s, 30 percent of the over-the-counter supplements you can buy in GNC are now on the banned list. Medical sports science changes with time. If you asked me, a fan about PEDs or steroids or any of those types of drugs in sports, I would tell you, I don't care. I don't know who was using what, and I don't care how they were affected. Just like in baseball with a lot of disputed charges, the list is out of control. So let's stop right there; let's run some tests. See what the affect is scientifically. You know, the test takes twenty players—give ten of them PEDs, give ten of them placebos—run the test, crunch the numbers, keep it anonymous. When they do that, we can have a real discussion about PEDs; break out the data only if MLB doesn't leak it first. Football handles the steroid issue better: they punish their players for violating but with less fanfare. I guess they are more sensitive too, considering the frequency of injury in their game, the healing process, the physical nature of the game what are the advantages and disadvantages, what makes you stronger versus what keeps you from getting hurt. Are we not searching for prevention? Use the science or are we as smart as we think we are?

Socioeconomically Speaking

The 1980s was a socioeconomically defining decade for black people in general.

The '80s brought AIDS, Ronald Reagan, junk bonds, crack, the war on drugs, the escalation of gang and gun violence, and the evolution of rap music; also the temporary breakdown of the family structure was catastrophic. It was two steps forward and five steps backward. We didn't lose a generation; we just had it slow down a bit.

People incarcerated for doing drugs; poverty begot violence and all the residual fallout affected the kids of the '80s because it affected the parents who persevered and came through it. These parents raised great kids who are successful and productive today. There is a gap where progress slowed and impeded growth, education, jobs— well-paying jobs are way below par. The economy is down on the low and lower middle class, and the economy is up in Wall Street. To sum it all up, the progress blacks made in the '60s and '70s took a hit in the '80s and got sidetracked and are still playing catch up. The 9/11 changed America—that horrible, vicious, evil, insane slaughter of innocent people by Bin Laden and his evil terrorist group. It started at least three wars, killed hundreds of thousands, injured and maimed many more. It's been twelve years, and we are still trying to close the book on that chapter in America by taking out the mastermind behind this heinous act, Bin Laden, and ending the wars and American occupation of Iraq and Afghanistan. Thanks to the president that inherited the mess Bush left, 9/11's effect on the economy happened in a lot of ways, most of it triggered by big businesses and corporations from the top to the bottom where there were major liquidations, downsizing of companies, claiming they are going broke because of the bad economy. On top of that, none of the states can balance their budgets. All of this in effect started the change in the landscape of the pay scale for the average American worker. Everyone is saying they have to cut, cut, cut. Businesses started slashing their payroll literally telling workers they have to take pay cuts if they want to keep their jobs. And what this became was a way to make a profit by cutting your work force in half and tripling up the work on the people left, while threatening them with their jobs, telling them you are lucky to have a job in today's economy. And they ran that play over and over again until they exhausted it to the point where there was nothing else to cut. The ironic thing is after 9/11, the groups taking major cuts from cities were the police and fireman first responders. During that period

CEO salaries increased by leaps and bounds. I worked in companies up front and witnessed the dismantling process, where the worker is put under pressure and over working them under the threat of losing their job. When the companies realized that they were able to do it, the process became the method; workers' salaries went down substantially. I was part of a job that changed ownership, and they came in with that slash and cut. Blame it on the economy caused by 9/11 plans going full steam. After two weeks, they called all the employees, about sixty people, for a meeting. And they said to everyone in the room, "You are fired at this time. Those of you who still want to work can reapply right away at the minimum wage." I was the warehouse manager making about $60,000 their offer to me was $27,000—a pay cut more than half. They said, "You can take that or go on unemployment for $450 a week." I said I will take the unemployment for $450, Alex (jeopardy style). The industrial complex taking a beating—it was like an epidemic. And of course, the politicians were doing their thing; nothing productive, more fucking up. Bush started off okay after 9/11 going where Bin Laden was. Afghanistan's fine, we had to get him and bust up the Taliban to avenge the Americans that were killed in that evil attack. Go get them, we're all in. At that point in time, the country was united like Pearl Harbor. Bush could have asked us to do anything; the

American people, politicians, Republicans and Democrats, and Independents would have followed Bush anywhere as long as we got the Taliban. Then we go over to Iraq looking for WMDs. That was the wrong move, more dead Americans and dead Iraqis. What happened to all the oil we were getting access to—that was the real reason or at least one of them. Bush was caught in lie after lie; it was buffoonery, chicanery and incompetence. Some $750 billion spent on two wars and no Bin Laden at the end of the Bush term. The Republicans were jumping off Bush's ship like the rats they are. Economy wrecked America in a depression; real estate market crashed and then the banks go down, AIG, etc. And dumped it all in the next guy's lap then obstruct any progress. That's why many people, including me, are so frustrated with politics and the process. Politicians ain't worth a shit and I mean it.

The race card, a phrase I have a problem with, if race comes out and it will. Don't panic with the race card issue; it's going to happen simply because racism does. Look, the race card is played when I walk into the room because you know I'm black, I can't hide that card in the deck—it's out there. You don't know if a lot of gay people are gay until they say it. You can't tell if a white person was a Jew or a German, French, Irish, or what until they tell you. But you know I'm black when you see me. I don't know what white people think when they see black people. You should size a person up on how they speak and relate to you, but some stereotype right from the beginning. A lot of white people don't care and judge people for who they are as it should be but unfortunately it's not because race is and always will be prevalent in America. That's just my opinion about the race card thing. Racism and the race card reported on a national scale where you see it on Fox News looking to debunk it line by line. They have a method of looking for angles to make it look like people involved are overreacting and playing the race card. White people have an extreme reaction to race and charges of racism; it's like paranoia.

They go into "I'm not a racist" mode by categorically denying that they are not racist and then get offended that it was even insinuated. Right there, my reaction is just "relax, white people, it's not that bad. Calm down because black people been experiencing real racism for a long time in some form or fashion." A lot of the time the race charge happens, it's more exploited by the media or people that are part of or involved in the situation. The ironic thing is there is racism going on every day that you don't hear about all over the country in people's everyday life. They just go on and deal with it. We all know that it's not right. But it happens, so be cool, relax people. Everything will be all right. It's just part of the process as the generations evolve through race and race relations. We are a society of civil human beings. Each generation has it's take on racism and race breaks it down in decades. People in their sixties are different than people in their forties, and the same with people in their twenties. Dave Chappelle talked about it in entertainment and sports, how the races collide like in life, people have to work together and respect. You have to be politically correct. Racism still runs deep for average people, and racism in today's society seems complicated, but it's not. At this point it's generational, socioeconomical, and a horrible history in this country. My father experienced it more than me, and my son Akheem experienced it less than me, and it should be less for his son. Different generations, we should learn from that and start to educate are children against racism.

Okay, whew, let's deal with the N word—that treacherous, historically dirty word, and where it stands today. Here's the rule: black people can say it, white people can't, and actually black people need to cut down their usage especially around white people. Black people can't help but throw it in white people's face because the word is the word. It has a life of its own, way out in the stratosphere. It has its own existence and a negative history that form the power and effect the word carries. So it's in your face with the music, in movies, and out on the streets, glorifying the word, allowing us to use it in all kinds of extreme in the lexicon of the current culture. But, regardless, the word is the word and the rule is the rule—we all know it. I don't care if it ends with an "er" or an "a"—it's the same thing, you can't change the letter "a" to change the meaning of the word. All that to me is total bullshit. Besides how many times you think when it's just all white people do they say the N word, who knows I would guess it's probably a few. You can't help it when you are singing your favorite rap song; it maybe in the lyrics. Singing along in your car you might do it.

I really do believe a lot of white people don't use the word and they teach their kids not to use it and are appalled by the word and the use of it. I use the word once in a while but not around white people, and I don't do so much around black people because I should not need to. If a word means something bad for 300 years, I don't think you can change it and make it okay. Let's try something. Everyone, stop using it—is that possible? Probably not. At least try to cut down if it's part of your vocabulary. When you say it, take a look why you said it, and you may start using it less if you take that approach . . . To each his own.

Police Stories

The police law enforcement, we need police to protect and serve to keep us safe. African American men have a different, let's say, *relationship* with the police. If you were to take a survey of black men from the ages sixteen to sixty-one and ask them if they had contact or confrontation with law enforcement, I would bet, without the results of the survey, the majority of them would say yes. Profiling exist black men are targeted unfortunately, that's the truth. Branded the usual suspect, it can't be denied. I have seen it up close and personal. Black men are commonly a criminal threat, that even some white people blame it on a black guy to divert the cops from looking at them by saying some black guy did it. How many times have you heard of a case where the white guy kills his wife and blames it on a black guy or a group of black guys who tried to rob them or a white woman getting carjacked and the black guy drove off with her two kids in the backseat. And then come to find out she drowned them, killed her own kids, tragic and sick. The automatic suspect is the black guy that police frequently press that button and play. I myself had more than several encounters with the police, and I am no way a criminal or criminal type. Hey, I am an upstanding citizen. Anyway, while driving a nice car, I was pulled over fourteen times in one year and got a total of two tickets. I said two, yes, two tickets; so it meant the other twelve times, they were just checking to see who I was. I had no criminal record, never been arrested. One time, I got stopped by seven police cars. They blocked me at the intersection, at least ten policemen with their guns out, drawing down. I was in a convertible with the top down. I raised my hands straight up, they snatched me out of the car and handcuffed me. At that time, I worked for the government, the Department of Defense, in the computer room as a digital computer mechanic. I worked on the Crypto equipment, one of the launching systems for nuclear submarines. I had to have a top secret clearance from the FBI that provided me with two pieces of federal pictured ID, plus my driver's license. In other words, I had a whole gang of IDs. So they checked everything, found out who I am—nobody, not a threat, just an upstanding citizen. Their excuse was I had a car like that of a drug dealer in the area, and they thought I was him. They did apologize and start addressing me as "Mr. Figg" because they were wrong, wrong, wrong again.

I could give at least four or five other incidents where they were wrong, and I could have been hurt or shot by making any wrong move. It's not nice to have a police or anyone point a gun at you. That is why I practice police educate. I try to teach to young men this thing. I call police educate the proper behavior to use when dealing with the police:

1. Be very polite, 2. Don't make any sudden moves, 3. Cooperate fully. If that don't work, put your hands behind your back and prepare to get handcuffed. In my case, like most for some reason once black guys get older, the police hassle them less, I guess less of a threat. Another police story sitting in the living room on the couch late one night about to fall asleep and then bam! The police kick in the door with his gun out talking about where did he go. My response was "Where did *who* go?" He said a young guy, a teenager, he was chasing him and he ran down the side of my house. The cop was convinced that the guy he was chasing ran inside my house. He said he had the right to search because he was after a f leeing suspect. He then called back up, and he and the other cops proceeded to search my home, thinking I am hiding someone. After finding nothing and realizing they were wrong, I also reiterated they were wrong again. The cop who kicked in the door was very upset and very rude and still accusing me of lying among other things.

We started arguing and almost came to blows. I could not believe it, me about to fight with a cop whose attitude was out of bounds. The other cop that separated us knew he was out of control because they did not do anything to me; and they pulled him away. They soon came back to me trying to smooth things over for their out of control, over-zealous partner. The dude was acting like the over-the-top cop on TV, the shield like the Michael Chiklis character, all jacked up to the tenth power. He was bugged eye and sweating profusely, it was surreal. Wrong again. The bad thing: it always starts with profiling.

The Trevon Martin-George Zimmerman case began with profiling and ended tragically. I'm not a lawyer but we all knew it was self-defense at the time of the shooting. They were in a fight, a life or death struggle; it was self defense. The prosecutor should have charged for the action that caused the reaction which resulted in the death of Trevon Martin. The action was profiling and continuing to follow Trevon after the police on the phone told him not to follow or confront him. His action caused the confrontation that turned into a fight. Zimmerman had a gun, and he provoked the confrontation and him being armed also inspired him to keep disobeying the police who was telling him to stop following and it ended up being self-defense but it was not a self-defense case. I blame that on the prosecutor for bringing the wrong charges. They left it to Zimmerman to prove exactly that it was self-defense. They were in a fight, that is what self-defense is. The bottom line is if Zimmerman was not armed with a gun, he would not have gone nowhere near Trevon. Imagine having a pistol makes you brave; it's just sad.

Education

Is America on the road to dumb down its future generations? Really are we witnessing the dumbing down of the American youth by our lack of funding and cuts and advocating for better education? Are we not the most powerful, most influential country in the world, and where do we rate on the scale on education—17th or 18th. We should want a sharp, highly educated, highly motivated future America. So that they aspire in the greatness of our country, or do we want a less-educated society with lower standards, setting the bar for just average and contentment for mediocrity, no higher learning, no critical thinking or get caught in the middle of this mass social media blitz, instant communication, reality show culture. Are we going to run the technology or let the technology run us? Split-second information sharing, a lot of short cuts, fool's gold. With the skyrocketing cost of education on the higher levels, how many of us get discouraged. It has to start early; K-12 process has to be successful with lofty goals in the curriculum to build a desire for higher education. Education is what we need and we need all we can get. Keep your kids on track; push them in that direction.

African American student affirmative action, do they need it? Hell, yeah! Can we get some more? We need all we can get. Give us all you've got. Let me tell you, these people who think the scale is fair, they are full of shit. You can run the numbers all kinds of different ways. Take the ratio of the higher educated vs. people in jail vs. the graduation rate for high school vs. black male and females vs. the total number of white on scholarship vs. total enrolment vs. the real monster, the cost or finance. Affirmative action helps it to go where it deserves. That dude Ward Connerly needs his butt kicked for his position on affirmative action. And he is an old school guy, he should know his perspective is way out of touch with black youth and opportunity, and realize we have to change the education culture to catch up, not just to see a few aspire but make it a goal for all too. Hell affirmative action helped Ward get to where he is. Boy, what an idiot. We need to get the high school graduation rate up, so we can get to the point of affirmative action being affirmative.

Gas

Do you think gas will go down under $3 in California? We just don't care about gas prices anymore. We are all programmed to be content and accepting of the process, where prices are set by the gas futures market based on projected and predicted events, such as an oil refinery not producing or refineries not scheduled to produce three months from now, will raise prices today because the oil flow will be affected in the future, therefore oil futures. Even things like the weather can affect oil futures market. The government can't do much because the market controls the gas. When the oil companies can raise gas up to over $5 a gallon, they make huge profits. What makes you think they are going to let prices go down lower than $3? That's why they base the amount on the futures market so they can fluctuate the cost and keep it high. That's why gas prices yo-yos once it gets close to $3; going down, they raise it back toward the $5 dollar mark and stay close to those boundaries so they make $30-billion-dollar profits. When they first started this latest round of gas shortage back in 2000-2002, the major oil companies saw huge profits, record-breaking. They saw that, and that's when we got the spike in oil barrel prices, they went from $50 to $150 a barrel. When they got a taste of that, it has been the norm ever since. And another thing, what happened to the oil from Iran, reason why we went there. The only one's benefiting from that was OPEC. I bet that gas never, ever goes down to $2 a gallon again, at least not in California.

Hey, what do you know, a good thing happened with gas. The price of gas dropped to $3 and under for a short time. All the gas OPEC and oil reserves have been hoarding have made the gas prices per barrel go down. I wonder if Obama would get credit for gas prices leveling on his watch, definitely not from the Republicans. Hell, no, absolutely not.

My Introduction to Politics

My first experience with politics was with my parents. My folks always watched the news; I had to be five years old. I can remember them being so upset that day President John F. Kennedy was assassinated. It's weird I can recall all of that and have a clear memory at that age. I was so young but I remember the news repeating over and over that he was dead, killed by an assassin's bullet; he was shot in the head in his car. I recall Dallas, they kept repeating Dallas and book depository. And later they had caught the guy who did it—Lee Harvey Oswald. I recall the experience being a collective shock; it affected everyone. I was a little kid and I felt it. I remember a few days later, Oswald getting shot on live TV, while watching with my family. Jack Ruby runs up and shoots him while they were transporting him. My father was like, "What in the hell is going on?" and at five years old, I'm taking all of these in the guy who kills the president, gets killed by another guy—it was stunning to me. My parents voted for and supported Kennedy and the fight for civil rights. His death looked like it would be a huge blow to equal rights. Lyndon Johnson, Kennedy's successor, he did follow through on the civil rights bill. I recall my parents watching closely what he did during his presidency. I later learned that Johnson was a shrewd, no-nonsense negotiator. He used the bully pull pit; they said he would twist arms and threaten to break them if they did not vote his way. Back to the assassination of Kennedy, to this day, with all the investigating and conspiracy theories, we still don't know what actually happened. Jack Ruby stopped all of that. Who knows what happened? That hole runs so deep and so dark it's been fifty years, and we still don't know the truth. That was just the beginning of the assassination decade. I recall hearing about Malcolm X getting assassinated. At that time, I had just recently found out who he was. I remember the adults around me were stirred up about how it happened, the shady characters involved, how he was killed by the Black Muslims. The other murders of the assassination decade, Martin Luther King and Robert Kennedy, those I remember way more vividly. They had a profound effect on me. It was like assassination was becoming the way of the world. It was like if you don't like someone's views or opinions, you just kill them, that was the solution. That was so crazy to me. What I remember about the MLK assassination was the sadness it brought. I recall a lot of people were crying everywhere. We went to school, the teachers and the students were crying. The principal of my elementary school was a personal friend of Dr. King, he was visibly shaken they dismissed school early that day. I knew of Dr. King from his "I have a dream" speech. I remember as a child, watching the news about the struggles in the south and asking my father why were they using fire hoses on those people and why were they setting the dogs on them and my father told they were fighting for their rights with Dr. King. And f lashing back when you listen to Dr. King speeches, up until he was killed, it was like he knew he was going to die soon because of the movement he was leading. When he says, "I'm not worried about anything. I'm not fearing any man because he had been to the mountain top," means he was aware of the evil forces closing in around him, even the FBI. J. Edgar Hoover's surveillance, they should have been protecting him instead of investigating him. He turned out to be one of the greatest civil rights leaders ever. And Dr. King's killer, James Earl Ray, shrouded in conspiracy, a patsy, another unclear story. To even off the decade, the tragic death of Robert Kennedy, a new hope for the country poised to carry on his brother's work cut down by a familiar word to me now the word assassin, yes, another assassin deflating the spirit and the hope of the entire nation. Sirhan Sirhan, another murderer, I don't know what his deal was. It was the decade of if "we don't like you, we will end your life." Your political belief and affiliation could get you killed, and as a kid, that made me pay attention. Watching those four individuals who died for their political beliefs resonates with me, no doubt. People who took a chance and really tried to make a change made the ultimate sacrifice.

Why I Hate Politics

Politics. In some cases you have to separate everything from politics, job, business, family, friends, sports, entertainment. It's hard to do but it has to be done. People always have differences and different opinions, that's life and there is a time and place for everything. People believe what they want to believe. Like when you form an opinion, you take the facts you have about it, and formulate and come to a conclusion on what you think. That's usually the process in having an opinion, and you know what they say about opinions, they are just like another part of your body, we all got them and they all stink. Now that's not true; all opinions don't stink but a lot do and enough of them really smell. Where you have to pay attention and that leads back to politics, where you kinda have to pay attention. Politicians do wheel a lot of power of city, state, government and in the community. No doubt, they have a direct effect on how the country we live in is run and you have to keep an eye on them in today's political gridlock at the highest level.

Let me tell you why I hate politics. Politicians ain't shit; half of them are in bed with big business, lobbyist steering the country to their interest. The politicians that do look out for the common people can't get anything done. Congress is horrible, the Supreme Court is going backward, and the Senate is inept. Congress and the Senate can handcuff the president, and now you have the infestation of the Tea Party making it even worse with more divisions and gridlock.

Just a hypothetical thought, say, Hillary Clinton won the Democratic nomination in 2008 and went on to become president, do you think there would be the creation of the Tea Party. Hell, no. The Tea Party was formed right after Obama was elected. Their first rally looked like a KKK meeting. It's funny how some corporations can bankroll and create so-called grassroots groups like the Tea Party that came out of nowhere. The GOP are carrying out their obstructionist plan by saying no to everything—no stimulus, no health care, no jobs bill, no to building infrastructure, improving roads, and investing in our cities, and even no to students and education. They are acting like they are all committed to cut spending. What a crock. They're so worried about the debt— give me a break. How many Americans are actually worried about the country's debt? They are worried about their *own* debt. We all know the United States will never, ever, ever, ever run out of money. Those are just a few things that have me at the peak of frustration over politics. Hey, at least Obama came in trying to get something done and is constantly roadblocked zero cooperation from the Republicans, I used to be a political news junkie; I always tried to keep up with political events. I call myself keeping up with the political atmosphere. The deeper I got, the more I see how fucked up politicians are, no matter to what party they belong. Some of the Republicans come out like they have their finger on the pulse of the public like they know what the average person is going through. They come out spouting some of the most incredibly crazy ideas ever. And people are so gullible, they vote against their own interest, like sheep being led to the slaughter. Example to this day, we have a crazy congressman Cruz from the Tea Party trying to kill the health care bill. The Senate is threatening to shut down the government. News flash assholes you already shut it down with all the procrastination Bohner and Mitch McConnel. These guys are always trying to rationalize bullshit with their nonsense. They really believe the crap that comes out their mouths. I used to watch the political shows on CNN MSNBC stream on the computer talk radio I tried watching Fox news they just lied a lot and manipulated stories. Hannity and O'Reilly, those dudes are straight scary. Fox

News they do have good presentation and packaging colorful they suck people in and fill them with propaganda Republican style the Republican station. They're okay when they do straight news, but anything political they slant it hard right. Whew Fox and friends are definitely not everyone's friend; fair and balanced, yeah, right. MSNBC the Democrat station does lean that way, but they don't twist stories or provide you with misinformation to make someone or why something looks bad. Some of the media really don't splash the story of which the real culprits are. They don't really focus on who is really causing the problem. Instead of just saying the Republicans are messing it up, they say both sides are at an impasse. If one side wants to ruin everything, how do you progress? It's really sad to say how the Obama presidency will go down in history. It will reflect how far we have come and how some people have really showed their true selves. It will reflect on society, how the lack of cooperation with this president and the Republican Party. We will look back and say the first black president went thru hell, trying to lead the country out of depression, two wars, and a whole list of problem left by the Bush administration. And the Republicans tried to block him every way that they could by sacrificing the American people. Sorry to say race will be involved, and people are going to say it is because he is black and unfortunately that is the truth, and that is a shame. Some off the antics the Republicans have done are things no president has ever experienced. Disrespectful Senate members calling him a liar while he was addressing them, open defiance, and rudely unwilling to negotiate, total obstruction. If the president likes something, they hate it no matter what it is. That is a bad, huge negative in American history. Blatant disrespect never experienced by any sitting president.

Last Rant

This is my last rant on politics. I can't help it, I'm just concerned about the country and the people in it. About fairness and what fair really is—not some contrived version of it used as a slogan but what is true equal opportunity for hard working people to prosper. This nation will always be strong and so on. And we can't let middle and lower class be collateral damage left from greedy, power-hungry corporation, CEOs and politicians in big business pockets, with no regard for common people. Ease up, Republicans and you too, Democrats, with hidden agenda on entitlement and social security. Do you really think that poor people are affecting your wealth and well-being? What happened to America, home of the brave land of the free, America lived up to the demands of your principles. What happened to industrial might, where we do have opportunity for prosperity and enough financial gain to take care of its own. You think people on welfare are going to break the country? Do you think they want to be there, they are because they want to eat. Welfare, unemployment, insurance, food stamps help people through the lean times to tide over to the next job. Yes, people want to work.

We must pay attention to the Supreme Court. These justices literally chart the course of America, creating policies that will affect the next twenty years. Affirmative action watch out. The Supreme Court swings with the majority of the Justice's party affiliations.

Music

Music. I love all kinds of music; the universal language music influences culture worldwide. Music is always changing; different styles come and go. Rock and roll in the fifties, soul and rock in the sixties and seventies, funk in the seventies and eighties, rap in the eighties and nineties. Pop and country have been around for decades.

Grunge rock, acid rock, hard core rock, all kinds of rock, all lead guitar-driven. Soul morphed into R&B. Some say the best music the music of the sixties and early seventies—Motown era. Everyone thinks the era they were raised and listened to music is the best. The great thing about music is the way it breaks through perceived racial lines. Long, long gone are the days when certain races were programmed to like certain music. All black people don't like hip hop and all white people don't like rock and pop, all Asian people don't listen to Asian music, same with Hispanic. Now the fusion or crossover as music changes as it always does. The fusion, as I call it, is a combination of pop, R&B, hip hop, rock, the mix of styles and genres pop can be mix with hip hop rock and R&B combined and separate fused together to create the sound in today's popular music. The crossover zone is the most lucrative hip hop music has passed over into the crossover. The crossover has many layers based on the popularity of the music or the artist and promotion juice. To sum it up, all kinds of people love all kinds of music. Older people think some of today's music sounds like crap, and younger people think they are full of it. Technology and music have greatly improved. You don't even need instruments or know how to play them. With the auto-tune, people don't even have to be a good singer. The technology can alter and adjust vocals to pitch perfect. Every generation thinks that their music is the best. The people who started soul music are in their seventies and the people who started rap are in their forties and fifties. So does your age determine your music taste? Yeah, some. Music is meant to push the envelope, and that's how it evolves. Some music has gone beyond pushing the envelope to kicking over the mail box. Rap, hip hop, took us to another level when profanity got involved; all bets were off that opened the door to say anything. The music got very provocative on different levels: violence, drugs, sex mayhem denigration of women, gangs, anti-gay, even racist rap. That doesn't mean rap music is bad—it's just a way of expression. Some of it has a message and some of it don't, some of it is meaningless bullshit and some not. The real first old school rappers did dirty raunchy rap. Rudy Ray Moore and Blowfly, most people probably never heard of them. NWA and Too Short changed it for me. The first time I heard NWA's first album N's with attitude. It was one of the most incredible things I ever heard. I was in a car with an incredible bumpin' sound system I was totally amazed and impressed; it truly was a scintillating experience.

I remember to this day, man, I was completely blown away. Yeah, it was that good a master piece of cursing rhythm and rhyme and power—it was fresh, it was different. They made a statement if you can believe that was. Fuck the police Ice cube straight killed it the funny thing today Ice cube came full circle playing cops in his film career. Today hip hop and music in general they say anything to the 10th power hip hop rap music changes its f low. Also, it has moved from gangster to ballin. There is a large market of sex songs about having sex, about women's body parts, and how they move; some vulgar, some funny, and some insulting. That's music evolving kickin' over the mail box. As far I rate the music today, I like the artist and producer Pharrell. I think he is on the pulse of great music today and right on point with what I like to hear. He understands how to keep that old school funk and soul combine it with today's R&B and hip hop and came up with his unique sound and style. He can take a talented artist who is good and make them the best that he can be. So on top of it, he took two white guys, Robin Thicke and Justin Timberlake, and made them into R&B award winners. That's how bad he is; he brings out the best in them.

The Movies

The movies. The great American and worldwide escapism into a vision on film a story a journey with some type of coherent conclusion the movies away to immerse yourself into a world to watch a story play out and adventure a dramatic journey a comedic ride a plot you can make sense of, overall you want to be entertained thrilled touched a rollercoaster ride you may want to be terrified you may want to be amazed some inspire a lot, disappoint some are great, and a lot are horrible. There are a lot of choices, like horror movies alone, you got your blood baths, supernatural, demon— passion, creepy, diabolical, paranormal, and a whole rash of vampire stuff. You got romantic vampires, emotional vampires, moody vampires, melancholic vampires—it's like a vampire overdose. Movie recycling, that's big. There are more and more remakes do overs revamps, recreations and repeats every ten to fifteen years— you see it *Spiderman, Superman* like three times, four different *Batmans, Total Recall,* and many more. Movies—there are so many, do you have a top ten? Most people who enjoy movies need to have a top twenty. There have been a lot of great movies some of my favorites are *Star Wars, Fight Club, Shaft's Big Score, The Chinese Connection, The Matrix, Godfather 2, Goodfellas, Rollerball, The Warriors Pulp Fiction Gladiator,* I can go on and on. In the '70s, there was a brief explosion of movies made, starred in, produced, and directed by black artists. They were labeled as black exploitation movies. That description did not make sense to me. I saw no exploitation, I saw a lot of pride in people in charge believing promoting unity. Yeah, that's right, I said unity. They were about uplifting and perseverance of living and creating the American, dream having the advantage of freedom in this country. On the other hand, those movies depicted the struggle against forces like racism and prejudice, so that meant the main foe in a lot of these movies was the White man. And there would be violent confrontations resulting in a conclusion that led to blacks and whites having a showdown. A lot of those movies ended like *Django Unchained,* where the blacks basically eliminate the white oppressor, ending in a spirited motivational victory and the black people ride off into the sunset after beating down the man. Those movies got shut down. I wonder why they were labeled as black exploitation. When they looked to me more like black revolution, I think that's the real reason they were eliminated. At that time to me I thought that blacks were exploiting instead of being exploited. Some were badly made, but they were made. There is a library of films from black A to black Z. The industry shut these movies down because they did not want them to get out of control, sounds like politics. Not all of the movies depicted blacks as Pimp's, Ho's drug dealers and drug addicts or thieves some were very true to life. I just think exploitation that description was too much. It was a period in history and the evolution of race and race relations and it's volatility in that time period was different race was way more of a hot button issue because of it prevalence. Movies have come a long way with the technology Blacks have come a long way also they create, own developed produce and direct and Samuel L. Jackson has been in every relevant movie for the last 20 years. Just an observation about TV you know on the major networks like CBS NBC ABC and FOX they don't have the black family sitcom anymore the last one was My Wife and Kids on ABC that void has been filled by cable networks TBS TNT the black networks BET TV one Oprah OWN network they create those shows Tyler Perry is huge it is great how he provides a platform for talented people to perform.

The News

Every day you turn on the news, you here about something heinous sickness and disgusting assaulting, killing, hurting people, and you say boy it's a lot of crazy people in the world and you would be right. Out of 6.5 billion people on the planet what at least on the low end 10 million crazies that's a lot of nuts some are in prison already some are not you may have passed a few on the street today for all you know. Now when I say crazy I don't mean people thinking they have been abducted by aliens or have mental problems I'm talking crazy like people out doing mayhem hurting folks, blowing up stuff, killing, maiming, rape, child abuse. All that stuff is crazy and if you are doing crazy thing like that then that means you are crazy. Like serial killers, mass murderers like Bin Laden, Charles Manson, Ted Bundy, Hitler's crazy ass for sure the unibomber, the columbine ass holes, and anyone else who kills innocent people. Crazy comes in all colors, shapes, and sizes.

They shoot up schools with innocent children or a movie theater full of people at a midnight premiere, with no regard for human life. That, to me, is what I consider crazy. Suicide bombers are crazy as hell. Anyone who would blow themselves up to take out innocent people are out of their mind. Terrorist commit those acts of violence and say, Allah told them to do it and it's God's will. No way is it God's will for anyone to kill innocent people, while blowing themselves to smithereens in the process. That is not the message, that is a wild interpretation of zealots and just flat-out crazy, we have some bona fide nuts we need to put under the Jail.

Equal Opportunity

Everyone has an equal opportunity to act like a fool, and what I mean by act like a fool is like just doing dumb shit, taking things to the extreme, morally compromising, irrational behaviour, just plain acting like a fool. Any person of any race or color can do it. That's why reality TV is so successful, they can put anyone on doing anything, and people will do anything searching for some kind of fame or whatever. Black people, white, Latin, Asians, Arabs, Jews, and everyone under the sun, acting a fool and doing dumb shit is an equal opportunity employer. They can create a reality show about any walk of life—a beauty shop, barbecue joint, nerds, police, doctors, bachelors, bachelorettes, dogs, cats, housewives, hillbillies, jersey, bad girls, good girls, bitches, flavor flav, honey boo boo and the duck dudes, you see what I'm saying. We can go on and on with this list, and it's all fair game. Acting a fool don't discriminate, it sucks a lot of people in. Hey, more power to anyone successful on reality TV, some of it is good and a lot of it is ridiculously bad and it just have you shaking your head going what the hell was that, but you keep on watching. You ever see a promo ad for a new reality show, and you know right off the bat that you're not watching that shit; matter of fact, that's what you say. Then that's when I question people's motivation to be on TV. And at the end you go, yeah, acting a fool on TV, doing dumb shit, equal opportunity, anyone can do it. And if you're the network, why not keep manufacturing all kinds of crap you never know what's going to work. Just throw it up against the wall and see if it sticks. And the fiscal and financial benefits, they don't have to pay writers or real actors production cost, casting—they save millions versus doing a sitcom or drama. Now the reality shows where they are building something or have a goal creating a business, those are good. The one with people behaving badly or acting stupid, those I have a problem with and I just don't watch them. How many times when you are talking to your friends or anybody and you just break out in a fight probably not too much. On some of those reality shows, it's like we are just waiting for the physical confrontation right on queue. guaranty women are the absolute worse as they build up in a cauldron of volatility, and the hostility begins, the sniping then insults, and here comes the punches, a melee, the confusion. There's the drama and nonsense and the shock. Wow, did we see that coming? Yeah, right, but was it entertaining? Yeah, it was, damn, and that's the hook. The spontaneous human reaction, and everyone who is on the show knows that the most controversial hell-raiser gets the most attention and rises above the pack and spins off into their new career; that is the main objective. Ramping it up for the camera has its benefits. So keep up the good work, or the bad work, whatever fits to clown or not to clown, that is the question. Everyone has an equal opportunity to act like a fool.

Ninety-nine Problems

The hip hop artist JZ has a rap song where he say he got ninety-nine problems and a bitch ain't one. I personally would like to change the bitch part to women I got ninety-nine problems and a woman ain't one. I like to believe that women are a major part of most men's life. They affect us deeply mentally and physically. They are God's greatest creation; they can be loving, dependable, reliable, and spiteful, all in the same day. The bottom line is that both sexes put each other through the ringer. But back to ninety-nine problems and a woman ain't one, you will have some problems. Men are definitely not perfect, far from it, but when we love a woman, we love hard, we care, we care about how you feel and what you are doing. The guys who have ninety-nine problems and a woman ain't one, how you do that I envy that. They are players for real or rich as hell, and they just bounce women in or out of their life. Women have the right to be suspicious and leery of men because of our track record of loving them and leaving them and making babies that some men don't take care of or have a relationship with. But on the f lip side, those ladies don't keep a man out of his kid's life just because you had a bad breakup and have a problem with the father. There are still good guys out there who take care of their own, regardless of what your best girlfriend is telling you. How great would it be if women and men always thought on the same level. When that works out, you build a strong and lasting relationship and make an effort not to argue about unnecessary things—it burns up too much energy. Stop complaining so much; stay positive. I love women, and good or bad; if it's not one of my ninety-nine problems, it is one of my ninety-nine concerns. Yeah, I got ninety-nine concerns and my woman is at least forty of them.

The Humor

You ever see something so funny you never forget it? The funniest thing I have happened many years ago in high school. It happened at an autoshop class in the annex building. The annex had a long corridor with a concrete f loor with water pipes that ran along the ceiling about ten feet in the air. There's this guy in class, let's call him Rob. Now Rob was a pretty sharp dresser. He rarely wore sneakers and he would mostly wear dress shoes or casual. One day, he came in with some brand new Converse basketball shoes on; they were gleaming white Chuck Taylors. And there's this thing about a new pair of Chucks; they had so much grip and traction you could run up a wall Bo Jackson style for real. Anyway Rob, thrilled with these new Chucks, was jumping around the whole period. He had so much spring from the shoes that he was leaping high in the air, trying to see how high he could jump, and he had some serious hang time. So as soon as the bell rings period over, time to go, Rob is the first one out of the shop—running and jumping in these brand new white Chucks. He ran into the hall at the annex where the pipes ran along the ceiling, he jumped in the air, grabbed the pipes and pulls himself up and f lips over. Now picture this: he is now facing the f loor that is ten feet down, his hands are between his legs holding the pipes; that is when he realized if he let go of the pipes, he would fall ten feet f lat on his face; and in that split second, he let go. Now the problem was his hands were between his legs upside down when he let go, so while he was falling he was trying to get his hands out to break his fall, it was like in slow motion as he tried to work that arm free as he fell and hit the ground hard splat. By that time, I was behind him when he hit the ground and the tips of his brand new white Chucks hit the ground. They kind of bounced hard like *boom! boom!* A few of us ran to check on him; we thought he was hurt. But he got up and he was smiling with this stupid look on his face; he was okay. When we saw that, we burst into hysterical laughter, I mean, we were rolling. It was like fifteen guys in the autoshop class, all running down the hall, howling in laughter. It was the all-time funniest thing I have ever seen. You had to see it to believe it, side-splitting hilarious. I think we laughed every day for about a month! One of the funniest things was the way the tips of the brand new white shoes bounced off the ground when he landed, and that dumbass smile he had on his face when he got up—that was it for me.

The real funny thing was when the toe part of the new Chucks bounced off the deck, that was hilarious. We all need to laugh. You need some levity in your life. If you're laughing doesn't that mean you're happy. My father was a funny guy; he was so cool with it because he was real subtle and way out in front of you with it and it was spontaneous. He was hilarious and low key, never got excited just mellow with it. Laughter coincides with being happy and bonding, that's what he taught us. One of the moments was the Jimmy story. I have seven brothers and sisters. That day my sisters Mildred and Darlene, a few cousins, my mother and I were together when my father came in and started telling us he killed the rat that was in the house. There were mice in the garage coming into the kitchen and my Dad was a rodent and insect executioner. Now while he was telling us, Mildred kept interrupting him asking him what rat was it. She kept going, "What rat was it, Dad, what rat was it?" he paused and looked at her and said, "His name was Jimmy, Mildred. The rat's name was Jimmy," he said it with this dead pan serious delivery. Everyone burst into laughter. It was so funny, the way he just casually said it was hell of funny. He would joke like that all the time.

Speaking of funny, the evolution of the black comedians affected the mainstream comedy, where they have contributed and elevated the standard in the scene of comedy like with Bill Cosby setting a standard, Richard Pryor changing the game, then Eddie Murphy came along and took comedy to another level. What made Eddie Murphy so good was he was the best of Cosby and Pryor combined. With himself and an edge from a new era changing the game again, inspiring and opening up opportunities for a whole new generation of black comedians: Chris Rock, Martin Lawrence, Robert Townsend, Keenan Ivory Wayans, and a whole list of successful comedians. Richard Pryor not only changed it for black comedians, he changed it for all. The way he incorporated storytelling in his jokes, his style, his delivery, and with the language, which is the foundation of comedians today.

In high school, I had a cool teacher. He brought in Richard Pryor's album, *That Nigger's Crazy*, and the assignment was just for us to listen. After school, we went right to the store and got the album. That's how funny it was. Richard Pryor changed the landscape for stand-up comedy.

Sports and Politics

Mixing sports and politics is like mixing oil and water. I don't know if it works. People get offended and there is a lot involved—business, personal, emotions, passion, sports and politics, never the two shall meet. I have an opinion on both so I have to do it. Okay here it is: sports is good politics is bad. That's real simple; case closed. In sports, there is a clear cut winner, you win, game over, on to the next. In politics, it doesn't matter what happens, win or lose, the bullshit goes on; and only a very few play fair. The people who screw it up screw it up because they can and they continue to get away with it because that's the nature of the beast they created. It is not supposed to be that way, but that's the way they made it—and there lies my frustration, I'm done with it. I will vote and keep my eye on it because that is what I do . . . so pay attention it doesn't cost a thing.

Now I love sports. It moves every day, always progressing and building. Ever since back when I was a little boy, my older cousins Lawrence and Ray started me in sports—baseball, basketball, and football. Really love those guys for that, and I also love them because they are family and that's what it's all about. I Love My Family. Some may look at this book like I am some type of black activist with some radical agenda. I am not about that. I am about black awareness, I'm about people awareness. Race comes up because it is an issue, that's all. Me, hey, I love everyone. It does not matter what color you are; as long as you act right, we're good. Respect—that is the key.

Family

Growing up, I would pay attention to older people and what they were saying. They are the people who had something, built very productive lives, and raised great families. It was like they were giving me their wisdom and knowledge of the life they experienced, schooling me on the right direction to take and how to progress, giving me an education, strong work ethic, dedication, and love of family, moral responsibility, respect, and just plain knowing right from wrong. Some young people listen and some don't. My advice: pay attention, either way young people get old and then they realize that they should have listened to what old Uncle Jimmy had to say. The family thing . . . everyone should invest in it. Why not when you are already there, you are in for better or worse, good or bad, the greatest investment of your life. By family I mean my family, your family. The life relationship immediate and all levels you build with family members. My family connection is just the way my parents molded and shaped it to be, where we all would carry on the same goal of keeping the love, the devotion, and respect it; and building on the tradition of the family unit, intact, staying attached for generations to come, fulfilling my parents' dream of family unity—I mean, siblings, aunts, uncles, nieces, nephews, cousins, first, second, third, fourth, whatever. We should stay connected. I would hope that everyone gets a chance many of us do to invest in the family. It takes patience, love, respect, and humility, and a whole lot more. Sometime you just have to find a way. My parents learned from their parents and so on.

In memory of my brother, Ronald Hill.

www.ingramcontent.com/pod-product-compliance
Lightning Source LLC
Chambersburg PA
CBHW050412290526
45786CB00003B/1235